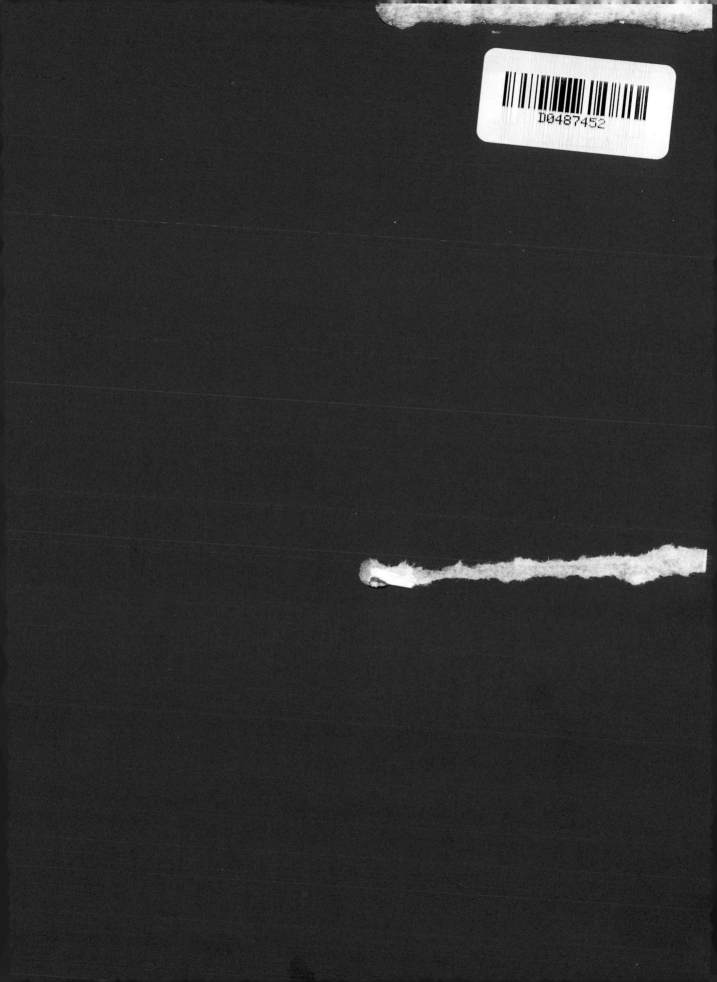

■ BRITISH HISTORY MAKERS ■

HORATIO NELSON

LEON ASHWORTH

CHERRYTREE BOOKS

A Cherrytree Book

Designed and produced by
A S Publishing

First published 1997
by Cherrytree Press Ltd
a subsidiary of
The Chivers Company Ltd
Windsor Bridge Road
Bath BA2 3AX

© Cherrytree Press Ltd 1997

British Library Cataloguing in Publication Data

Ashworth, Leon
  Horatio Nelson. – (British history makers)
  1.Nelson, Horatio Nelson, Viscount – Juvenile literature
  2.Admirals – Great Britain – Biography – Juvenile literature
  3.Napoleonic Wars, 1800-1815 – Naval operations – Juvenile
    literature
  4.Great Britain – History, Naval – 19th century – Juvenile
    literature
  I.Title
  359.3'31'092

ISBN 0 7451 5290 2 (Hardcover)
ISBN 0 7540 9013 2 (Softcover)

Printed and bound in Italy by New Interlitho, Milan.

Acknowledgments

Design: Richard Rowan
Editorial: John Grisewood
Artwork: Malcolm Porter
Photographs: *Barnaby's Picture Library* 28/29 top, 29 bottom left *The
Bridgeman Art Library* 8/9 bottom (Christie's Images), 9 top left (Agnew &
Sons, London), 10 top (Agnew & Sons, London), 11 bottom (Bonham's,
London), 13 bottom (Yale University Art Gallery), 24 top (Lauros-Giraudon),
25/25 bottom (Phillips Auctioneers) *The Mansell Collection* 16 bottom *Mary Evans
Picture Library* 17 top right *National Maritime Museum* 4 top & bottom, 5 (&
cover), 6 top & bottom, 7 top left & right, 9 top right, 10 bottom, 11, 12 (& 1),
12/13 top, 14/15, 16, 17 top left & bottom (& cover), 18, 19, 20/21, 22/23, 25 top
& centre, 26/27 (& cover) 27, 28 bottom left, 29 bottom right

CONTENTS

■ ENGLAND'S ADMIRAL ■

ADMIRAL HORATIO Nelson is the greatest of all England's sailor heroes. The men he led followed him cheerfully and without question. He won important sea battles during the Napoleonic Wars against the French. His love for Lady Emma Hamilton was famous. And he died fighting at Trafalgar – the most famous sea battle in British history.

From the time he first went to sea, Nelson believed he would be an admiral and command a fleet in battle. He spent most of his life at sea in wooden sailing ships. He was often seasick and he was badly wounded – losing his right arm and the sight of his right eye. Even when in pain and unhappy, he was sure that he would win the biggest battle. His men respected and loved him: 'the Nelson touch' inspired loyalty.

NELSON'S LIFE

1758 Born.
1770 Enters the Royal Navy.
1771 Goes to sea as a midshipman.
1773 Sails to the Arctic.
1777 Becomes a lieutenant.
1778 Commands his first ship.
1787 Marries Frances Nisbet.
1794 War with France. Loses sight of his right eye during an attack in Corsica.
1797 Fights in the battle of Cape St Vincent. Leads attack on Santa Cruz, Tenerife, is wounded and has his right arm amputated.
1798 Defeats the French fleet in battle of the Nile.
1801 Battle of Copenhagen against the Danish fleet.
1803 Made commander-in-chief of the British Mediterranean fleet.
1805 Defeats French and Spanish fleets at Trafalgar. Dies.

▲ The signature of Horatio Lord Nelson, England's greatest naval hero.

▼ A picture by Nicholas Pocock in which all of Nelson's most famous ship are shown at anchor at Spithead. HMS *Victory,* Nelson's flagship at the battle of Trafalgar, is on the far right. Behind her is the *Captain,* which he commanded at Cape St Vincent. To the left is *Elephant,* his flagship at Copenhagen, *Vanguard,* his flagship at the battle of the Nile, and *Agamemnon,* his first big ship.

QUOTES

'He is so good and pleasant that we all wish to do what he likes, without any kind of orders'.
Captain George Duff of the *Mars*, one of Nelson's ships at the battle of Trafalgar.

'I will be a hero and, confiding [trusting] in Providence, I will brave every danger'.
Nelson, recovering from sickness in India, 1776.

◀ **This portrait of Nelson was painted immediately after his victory at the battle of the Nile, which took place in 1798.**

■ THE PARSON'S SON ■

HORATIO NELSON WAS born on 29 September 1758. Horace, as he liked to be called, was the sixth of 11 children born to the Reverend Edmund Nelson and his wife Catherine. Three children died as babies. The family lived in the rectory at Burnham Thorpe, a small village in Norfolk not far from the sea.

NELSON'S MOTHER

Nelson's mother's family were called Suckling, and among her ancestors was Sir Robert Walpole, Britain's first prime minister. This made her rather grander than Nelson's father, whose grandfather had been a baker. She died in 1767 when Nelson was only nine years old.

A COUNTRY CHILDHOOD

As a country parson, Nelson's father was not a rich man. He grew his own vegetables to help make ends meet. Yet he was able to keep two menservants, and paid village women

▲ Nelson at the age of eight.

▼ The Old Rectory at Burnham Thorpe, Norfolk, where Nelson was born and lived as a child. He could be the small boy waving a flag in the picture.

to cook, clean and care for the younger children. The family lived quietly. News from outside travelled slowly, for letters and newspapers had to come over dusty roads from London by coach and wagon.

BOYHOOD HEROES

The most exciting news of Nelson's boyhood was of Britain's war with France – the Seven Years' War (1756-1763). His boyhood hero was General James Wolfe, who captured Quebec in Canada from the French but died at the moment of victory. He read of battles in India won by Robert Clive, and of other British victories at sea.

▲ Nelson's mother died when he was only nine. His grandmother helped to look after him and saw him off to join the navy.

▶ Nelson's father was a kind but strict man. It must have been hard for him to cope on his own with so many children.

RULING THE WAVES AND THE WORLD

IN NELSON'S day, Britain, France, Spain and Portugal all had empires in far-flung parts of the world. From their colonies they earned great wealth which gave them power at home in Europe, so they were constantly trying to outdo each other. To gain and manage the colonies, naval power was essential. The navy transported troops to fight on land, and protected the overseas possessions and merchant ships. Holding on to colonies and to power was not always easy. In Nelson's lifetime, Britain was to fight a war against its own subjects in America, while France was to experience a revolution that brought Napoleon Bonaparte to power, and plunged Europe into war.

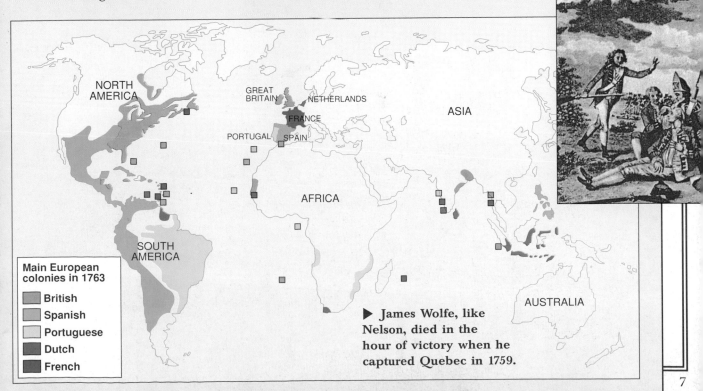

Main European colonies in 1763
- British
- Spanish
- Portuguese
- Dutch
- French

NORTH AMERICA
GREAT BRITAIN
NETHERLANDS
FRANCE
PORTUGAL
SPAIN
ASIA
AFRICA
SOUTH AMERICA
AUSTRALIA

▶ James Wolfe, like Nelson, died in the hour of victory when he captured Quebec in 1759.

■ SCHOOLDAYS ■

EDMUND NELSON was a pious but strict father. The children had to sit up straight at table, with their backs not touching the chair. Horatio was soon sent away to school, as was usual with the sons of clergymen.

Horatio attended three schools in Norwich, Downham Market and North Walsham. At this last school, he is said to have crept out at night to pick pears from the headmaster's garden. He gave the pears to his friends, and enjoyed their admiration.

AN AMBITION TO DO WELL

Two of Nelson's brothers became clergymen. Another worked as a clerk in the Navy Office in London. His sisters married and made their own homes. But Horatio had his sights set on the world beyond England. Days spent watching ships sailing along the coast near home may have made him dream of the sea and joining the navy. He had an uncle – his mother's brother – who might

EVENTS

1768-71 James Cook begins his first voyage to explore the Pacific. The Royal Academy of Arts is founded in London, with painter Sir Joshua Reynolds its first president. First edition of the Encyclopaedia Britannica.
1769 Napoleon Bonaparte, future emperor of France, is born.
1770 In America, British soldiers fire on a crowd in Boston – a sign of trouble to come.

NAPOLEON

NAPOLEON Bonaparte (right) was born 11 years after Nelson, in 1769. While Nelson's boyhood was peaceful, Napoleon's was full of drama. Napoleon was born on the Mediterranean island of Corsica, where his father was fighting for its independence from France. By 1804 Napoleon had made himself emperor of France and master of Europe. The biggest block to further French victories was Britain's Royal Navy and Nelson – the parson's son from Burnham Thorpe.

help. In 1770 Captain Maurice Suckling was made commander of a 64-gun battleship. Britain was making ready for a possible war with Spain. Nelson asked his brother William to write to their father, who was staying in Bath. 'Tell him I should like to go to sea with my uncle Maurice'. Nelson had decided where his destiny lay.

▼ A coastal scene from Nelson's time. The boy learned about the sea and ships while watching and talking to local fishermen, but it was the great sailing ships that maintained Britain's power and wealth that stirred his imagination.

■ THE YOUNG MIDSHIPMAN ■

NELSON WAS ONLY 12. His uncle Maurice joked: 'What has poor Horatio done, who is so weak, that he should be sent to rough it out at sea?' It was no joke. Life at sea in the 1770s was tough. All the Nelson children seem to have been rather delicate and Nelson was small for his age. He might not survive.

HIS FIRST SHIP

Still Nelson would go. In 1771 he left Norfolk. His father went with him as far as London, and then said goodbye as the boy took the stagecoach for Chatham, in Kent. There, in the naval dockyard, Nelson found his uncle's ship. Workmen were busy patching her up in case of war.

Uncle Maurice was not yet on the ship, so Nelson had to make himself at home as best he could. A kindly officer bought him dinner at an inn. That night he slept in a hammock for the first time, in the overcrowded cabin he shared with the other midshipmen.

▲ Captain Phipps commanded the expedition to the Arctic in 1773, in which Nelson served on the *Carcass.*

▼ Nelson fearlessly raises his gunbutt to club a wounded polar bear. He was determined to take the animal's skin home as a trophy. Luckily for him, a cannon shot from the ship scared the bear away.

A MIDSHIPMAN'S LIFE

THE MIDSHIPMEN on a warship were junior officers, but they could be any age from 13 to over 40. As a newcomer, Nelson got the worst jobs. He worked alongside the ordinary seamen (right), learning to climb to the mast top, to haul on ropes and sails, and handle a small boat. The midshipmen breakfasted like the ordinary sailors on 'burgoo', a thick porridge, and dished out soup and stew from a huge tin dish. They lived in a cheerful muddle. There was no privacy and no one was very clean.

▼ A view of Greenwich and Deptford in London, showing the Royal Dockyard in 1789. Over 12,000 workers were employed in building and repairing the navy's huge fleet of over 800 ships, making this Britain's biggest industry.

WIDENING HORIZONS

Nelson did not stay long aboard the battleship. There was no war. So, to give the lad a taste of the wide ocean, Captain Suckling sent him on a merchant ship to the West Indies. Nelson was seasick crossing the Atlantic. All his life, he was seasick on any vessel smaller than a battleship. But he loved life at sea.

Nelson was lucky to have his uncle to help him. In 1773, now almost 15, he joined an expedition to the Arctic. Other young officers were left with boring jobs ashore. No sooner was he back from the Arctic than he was sailing in a new ship to India.

INDIA, SICKNESS AND WAR

Nelson spent almost two years in the East, until he became sick at the end of 1775. He was so ill that he had to be shipped home. During the six-month voyage, he slowly regained his strength. He landed at Woolwich to hear the news that Britain was at war.

■ TAKING COMMAND ■

BRITAIN WAS AT war with its own subjects, people who had settled in America and founded colonies on the east coast. The American colonists had rebelled against the British government. They said it was unfair for Britain

▶ The newly promoted Captain Horatio Nelson looked healthy but was in fact often ill. He suffered bouts of yellow fever and scurvy, as well as sea-sickness.

THE ROYAL Navy in the 1700s was always short of men. Some men went to sea willingly, hoping for adventure and treasure. But many sailors were at sea only because they had been seized by the press-gang – a kidnap squad sent out to gather recruits (below). Men

vere hauled off merchant ships
t sea or in port. Others were
rabbed from the street or
avern – often drunk or
nconscious. The hapless men
woke to find themselves at
ea.

to tax the American colonies when they had no say at all
in how Britain was governed. The Americans had no navy
to threaten Britain. But France and Spain did, and these
two countries backed the American rebels. The Royal
Navy had to protect merchant ships and stop aid from
reaching the Americans.

PROMOTION AND HIS FIRST SHIP

In the spring of 1777, Nelson passed his examination to
become a lieutenant. He wrote to his brother William, 'So
I am now left in the world to shift for myself, which I hope
I shall do . . .'

The new lieutenant was gaining experience. He sailed on
convoy escort to Gibraltar and led a press-gang to collect
recruits for the fleet. Captain Suckling had died, but
Nelson had caught the eye of senior officers. In 1778 he
was made commander of a small warship called *Badger*,
and sailed to the Caribbean.

AN ILL-FATED MISSION

Nelson's orders were to lead a land expedition through the
jungles of Nicaragua. He was to attack a Spanish fort and
seize all the gold he could find. The mission ended in near-
disaster: local guides ran away, and seamen hauling boats
and guns overland became exhausted and sick. Nelson
showed courage and determination, but it was not enough.
He was taken back to Jamaica suffering from yellow fever,
and complaining (as he often did) that he was very ill.

The Boston Tea
arty of 1773 was
n early incident
the American
evolution. The
olonists objected
paying taxes to
ritain for goods
nded in America.
isguised as
ative Americans,
ey threw cargoes
tea overboard
to Boston
arbour.

■ NEW EXPERIENCES ■

THE WAR IN America was going badly for Britain. But it was being lost by politicians and soldiers, not by sailors. Nelson went off to holiday in Bath. He was still sure that he would command a fleet.

Nelson's next voyage took him north to the Baltic Sea. He sailed in the *Albemarle*, a captured French ship. The French built the finest warships of the day, and the Royal Navy had a number of French vessels. Nelson fell ill with scurvy, a disease caused by poor diet that affected many seamen in the 1700s. Then, he sailed to Canada and saw Quebec, the fort-city where his boyhood hero James Wolfe had died.

A USEFUL FRIEND

Nelson met Prince William (later King William IV) who was also in the navy. The young prince thought Nelson quaint for a captain – very young-looking, with his lank hair tied back, and wearing an old-fashioned waistcoat. Nelson thought the prince would be a useful friend in high places.

EVENTS

1781 *British army surrenders to the Americans at Yorktown.*
1783 *William Pitt becomes prime minister. First manned balloon flight in Paris.*
1784 *Nelson sails for the West Indies.*
1787 *Nelson marries Frances Nisbet.*
1788 *First British settlement in Australia.*
1789 *Start of the French Revolution. Mutiny on HMS* Bounty.
1792 *First demonstration of gas lighting.*

◀ Nelson met and became friendly with Prince William Henry, the future King William IV (the 'sailor king'), shown here as a midshipman.

▶ Nelson leaves the *Lowestoff* in rough seas to board a captured American ship in November 1777, during the American Revolution.

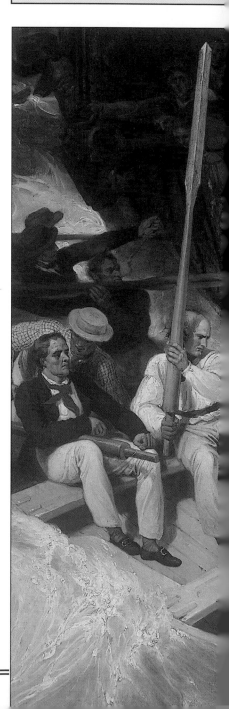

▲ Pictures that Nelson (left) and Cuthbert Collingwood made of each other in 1785. After meeting in the West Indies, the two young officers became lifelong friends and rose to be admirals.

SURE OF HIMSELF

Deciding he must learn French, Nelson spent some time in France, where he also enjoyed the company of English girls he met. Then he was ordered to the West Indies, to help prevent trade with the newly independent Americans. Nelson was so keen on this task that he upset local merchants and one island governor, who asked whether such a young officer knew what he was doing. Nelson retorted that 'he had the honour to be as old as the prime minister of England' (William Pitt, who was only 24).

MRS NELSON

On 11 March 1787, Nelson married Frances Nisbet, a doctor's widow who kept house for her wealthy uncle on the Caribbean island of Nevis. She had a small son, Josiah. The wedding took place on the island. Then the new family returned to England.

◀ Nelson's wife Frances (Fanny) Nisbet was used to the warm Caribbean. She and her five-year-old son found their first Norfolk winter cold and dull.

Norfolk winters came as a shock to Mrs Nelson, who was used to tropical warmth. Shivering, she stayed in bed, wrapped in curtain material. Downstairs, Nelson studied sea charts, browsed through books about the sea, or read the newspaper to his father, whose sight was now weak. Home life bored Nelson, who was no gardener or sportsman. The countryside in winter usually gave him a cold. He was restless, waiting for action. Great events were shaping.

■ INTO ACTION ■

IN 1793 NELSON took command of his first big battleship, the 64-gun *Agamemnon*. With him was his new servant, Tom Allen. Nelson's stepson, Josiah Nisbet, now 13, also joined the ship. After five years ashore, Nelson was happy to be back at sea.

NAPLES

Nelson sailed to the Italian port of Naples, where his ship anchored in the great bay beneath Mount Vesuvius. The king of Naples was needed as an ally in Britain's war against France. Nelson met the king and Sir William Hamilton, the British ambassador. The ambassador's attractive wife, Emma, was 'a young woman of amiable manners', wrote Nelson in a letter to his wife.

BATTLE SCARS

Nelson soon found the action he wanted. While fighting the French off the island of Corsica, he was hit by stones and splinters from a bursting cannon ball. His right eye was badly damaged; after this, he could see only light and dark with it.

In the scorching Mediterranean heat, Nelson made his sweating gun crews practise their shooting. This training had its reward when two French ships were damaged and captured.

Nelson felt the navy was not doing enough. He hoped that Admiral Sir John Jervis, newly in command of the British fleet, would win the much-needed victory.

CAPE ST VINCENT

On 14 February 1797, the British fleet met a larger Spanish fleet near Cape St

▶ **Sir William Hamilton, the British ambassador to Naples. His young wife, Emma, fell in love with Nelson and later set up home with him.**

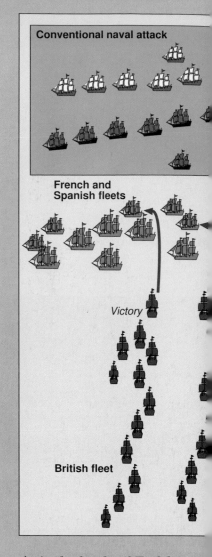

Conventional naval attack

French and Spanish fleets

Victory

British fleet

▲ **At the battle of Trafalgar Nelson attacked in two lines, s cutting off the enemy centre before the leading ships could get near enough to help. This was a brilliant tactic. In classic 'old' sea battles (top) the fighting fleets drew up in line facing each other and fought broadside to broadside.**

SHIPS OF THE LINE

THE BIGGEST warship o Nelson's time was the shi of the line – so named becaus fleets usually sailed into battle in a line. Ships were 'rated' by the number of guns and men they carried: a first-rate vessel carried over 100 guns and up 900 men. Smaller ships called frigates and sloops scouted to find the enemy and carried messages.

▲ King Louis XVI executed by guillotine in 1793 during the French Revolution. So began the 'reign of terror', during which France declared war on Austria, Britain and Prussia.

◄ Admiral John Jervis commanded the British fleet that roundly defeated the Spanish at Cape St Vincent in 1797. He greatly admired Nelson.

▼ Nelson leads a boarding party on to the *San Josef* during Spain's defeat in battle off Cape St Vincent in 1797. His part in the victory made Nelson the talk of the navy.

Vincent, off the southwest tip of Portugal. Spain was on the side of France. Jervis attacked.

Nelson – now on the 74-gun *Captain* – took his ship out of the line, drawing heavy gunfire from the enemy. The badly damaged *Captain* crashed into a Spanish ship and Nelson led his men in hand-to-hand fighting with swords and pistols. They captured the enemy ship, then boarded another.

A week later, Nelson was made a rear-admiral.

■ WOUNDED IN BATTLE ■

THE NAME OF Nelson was on everyone's lips, and people stopped him in the street to shake his hand. The young admiral was soon to earn further honours. In July 1797, in his latest ship, the 74-gun *Theseus*, Nelson attacked the Spanish port of Cadiz. During the hand-to-hand fighting, a brave shipmate twice parried sword thrusts that might have killed Nelson.

NELSON LOSES HIS ARM

Two weeks later, Nelson was fighting off Tenerife in the Canary Islands, then a Spanish fortress. Nelson and his men rowed ashore in small boats. The Spanish fought bravely. During the landing, many sailors died and Nelson's right arm was shot through.

The British gave up. Some officers ate a quiet dinner with the Spanish, as both sides gathered their dead and wounded. That night, the ship's surgeon cut off what was left of Nelson's arm. He was given the drug opium to ease the pain, but was back at work within the hour. Struggling to hold the pen in his left hand, he wrote gloomily, 'the sooner I get to a very humble cottage the better

▲ This picture of Sir Horatio Nelson, now a rear-admiral, was painted in Naples in 1799, shortly after the battle of the Nile.

EVENTS

1797 Nelson attacks Cadiz in Spain and Tenerife in the Canary Islands (July) and returns to England (September). Austria surrenders to Napoleon (October).
1798 Nelson joins Vanguard (March).

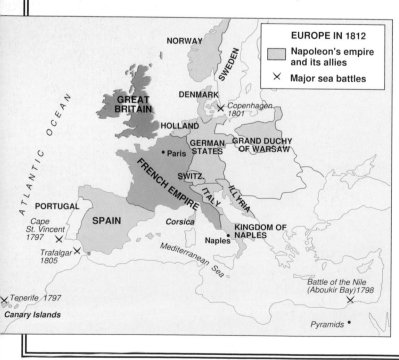

EUROPE IN 1812

Napoleon's empire and its allies

× Major sea battles

NORWAY
SWEDEN
DENMARK
× Copenhagen 1801
GREAT BRITAIN
HOLLAND
GERMAN STATES
GRAND DUCHY OF WARSAW
• Paris
FRENCH EMPIRE
SWITZ
ITALY
ILLYRIA
ATLANTIC OCEAN
PORTUGAL
Cape St. Vincent 1797 ×
SPAIN
Corsica
KINGDOM OF NAPLES
Naples •
Trafalgar 1805 ×
Mediterranean Sea
Battle of the Nile (Aboukir Bay)1798 ×
× Tenerife 1797
Canary Islands
Pyramids •

SURGERY AT SEA

SHIPS' SURGEONS operated on wooden tables, painted red (so the blood would not show). They used knives and saws to amputate legs and arms. In some cases a wooden 'peg leg' could be fixed to the stump. Wounded men were given rum or opium to make them drowsy and dull the terrible pain while the surgeon was at work. Nelson complained that the coldness of the knife was painful, and suggested that surgeons heat their instruments.

nd make room for a better man . . .'.

IR HORATIO

When Nelson returned to England, he was made a
night of the Order of the Bath. He now had enough
honey to buy a large house in the country. But his
rm healed slowly. People meeting him were shocked
y his grey hair, bad teeth and thin face.

Time for rest at home was brief. In
March 1798, Nelson was back at sea in the
Vanguard. The French had
athered a fleet and an
rmy led by the young
eneral Bonaparte. An
vasion was coming. But
here? Nelson was to
ek out the enemy and
ring them to battle.

▼ Nelson wounded at
Tenerife in the Canary
Islands. As he stepped
ashore at Santa Cruz
harbour to seize
Spanish ships – and in
the act of drawing his
sword – his right arm
was shattered by a
musket ball. He was
rowed back to his
flagship and that night
the arm was
amputated at the
elbow.

FIRST GREAT VICTORY

THE BRITISH FLEET lost touch with the French when their ships were scattered by a gale that damaged Nelson's ship. As soon as the repairs were made, Nelson set out eastward, searching the Mediterranean. Where was Napoleon going to land? Nelson and the British government both guessed: Egypt. Nelson duly found the French warships anchored in Aboukir Bay, near Alexandria. Napoleon was ashore. He had already beaten the Turks and Egyptians at the battle of the Pyramids. Now it was Nelson's turn.

THE BATTLE OF THE NILE

The water in Aboukir Bay was shallow and daylight was fading, but Nelson ordered his ships to sail boldly towards the French. Guns flashed in the darkness. Nelson's head was grazed by gunfire but, bandaged, he returned to the deck. After a 12-hour battle, the burning French flagship *L'Orient* exploded. The 'glorious victory' left Napoleon's army stranded in Egypt.

EVENTS

1798 Irish nationalists rebel against British rule in Ireland (May-June). Napoleon wins the battle of the Pyramids (21 July). Nelson wins the battle of the Nile (August) and is made Baron Nelson of the Nile (November).
1800 Robert Fulton, an American inventor, shows off his submarine Nautilus *to the French Navy. Washington D.C. becomes the new capital of the United States of America. Alessandro Volta makes the first electric battery.*

A SAILOR'S DAY

THE DAY AT sea began at 4 o'clock. Hammocks, slung from hooks between the guns, were stowed away. Breakfast of oatmeal porridge was washed down by 'Scotch coffee' (burnt biscuit mixed with boiling water). Dinner at noon was usually boiled salt pork or beef, with ship's biscuit followed by a plain boiled pudding or duff. The men drank beer or grog (rum weakened with water), since

▲ Nelson celebrates with his crew after the battle of the Nile.

water in wooden barrels soon went bad. Biscuits often had weevils (insects) in them, and a man nibbling cheese (a rare treat) kept an eye out for wriggling worms. Supper was biscuit and pea soup. During the day, the gunners practised firing their cannon. Seamen scrubbed decks and scrambled aloft to set or bring in sails, or drilled in fighting with cutlasses (swords) and muskets.

ENGLAND'S HERO

Nelson was made a baron and granted a yearly pension of £2000 (then a huge sum) by the government. Bonfires blazed and bells rang. Pictures of Nelson were sold from street barrows, songs were sung about him, and a dance was named 'Vanguard'. The heroic admiral was in no hurry to return home. His ship needed repairs, and he felt tired and ill. He decided to revisit Naples.

WELCOME TO NAPLES

Lady Hamilton greeted the news of the battle by first fainting and then riding through Naples wearing a 'Nelson and Victory' headband. She welcomed the hero with open arms and gave a grand party for his birthday. But the celebrations were cut short. The French and their allies were coming! Mobs jeered in the street as the king of Naples and his guests fled to Nelson's ship and sailed for Sicily. The grateful king gave Nelson a new title: Duke of Bronte (a town on the slopes of Mount Etna). After this, he always signed his name 'Nelson and Bronte'.

▲ Nelson kept a copy of this portrait of Emma Hamilton in his cabin aboard ship.

▼ The battle of the Nile. The French fleet lies at anchor in Aboukir Bay. As dusk and Nelson's ships approach, the French open fire.

■ BRITAIN VERSUS NAPOLEON ■

BY 1801, BRITAIN felt alone against Napoleon, who was master of France and much of Europe. It seemed that Russia, Prussia, Sweden and Denmark might join with Napoleon. Nelson's thoughts, however, were on personal matters. He and his wife were no longer living together and in January 1801 Lady Hamilton had a baby daughter – named Horatia, after her father.

TURNING A BLIND EYE

This event delighted Nelson. But he was impatient for action. He was pleased to sail to Denmark, to attack the Danish fleet in port at Copenhagen. The enemy ships were defended by guns on shore, but Nelson led the British ships in close to bombard them. Hyde Parker, the fleet commander, signalled him to break off the attack. Nelson put his telescope to his blind eye and said, 'I really do not see the signal'.

Nelson called Copenhagen his hardest battle. After three hours, the two sides agreed a truce. Nelson

▲ Horatia, daughter of Nelson and Emma Hamilton, with her rocking horse in the garden at Merton in Surrey where Nelson and Emma set up home in 1802.

A watercolour of the estate and country house at Merton that Emma Hamilton converted into a mansion.

A visiting card, a single left-hand glove and a combined knife and fork used by Nelson after he lost his right arm.

visited wounded sailors and met a man who had lost an arm, like him. He said with a smile, 'Well Jack, you and I are spoiled for fishermen'.

A COUNTRY GENTLEMAN

Britain and France made peace in 1802. Nelson and Lady Hamilton set up home at Merton Place in Surrey, a 100-year-old country house. Nelson could afford to take care of his two sisters and of family servants, including James Price, a black man who had worked for his uncle Maurice. Nelson made his first speech as a member of the House of Lords. It seemed his sailor's days might be behind him.

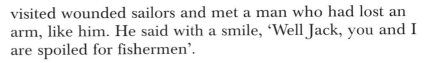

▼ Danish (left) and British ships in action at the battle of Copenhagen.

BATTLE AT SEA

WHEN lookouts spotted enemy ships, drummer boys beat 'to quarters'. This was a signal understood by everyone. Sails and decks were soaked with buckets of water, so they would not catch fire easily. Wet sand was scattered so men would not slip on the decks. The cannon – normally roped down, to stop them rolling about – were freed and the gun ports (window-like openings in the ship's side) were opened. Out of each one, a cannon pointed, with its gun crew ready. The galley fire was put out and the surgeons prepared to deal with the wounded and dying. Everyone on board was silent. In six minutes the ship was ready for battle.

■ BEFORE TRAFALGAR ■

IN MAY 1803, the brief peace ended. Britain declared war on France. After Horatia's christening, Nelson travelled to Portsmouth to prepare for battle again. He was the new commander-in-chief, and had a new ship, the *Victory*.

The fleet spent much of 1804 waiting for the French ships to leave port. By the end of the year, Spain had joined the war. Nelson knew he would face a stronger and combined enemy.

FIND THE ENEMY

No French army could land in Britain while the Royal Navy kept watch on French ports. Nelson spent almost two years (June 1803 to July 1805) at sea. He ate little and slept badly, often rising in the dark to walk on deck in his stockinged feet.

In the spring of 1805, Admiral Villeneuve, the French commander, led his fleet across the Atlantic Ocean to the West Indies. Nelson followed but Villeneuve slipped back homeward. By August, both the French and Spanish fleets were in the Spanish port of Cadiz.

THE BATTLE NEARS

Nelson enjoyed a month at home in

▲ Napoleon Bonaparte crowned himself emperor of France in 1804. He planned to invade England, if only his fleet could decoy the British ships away long enough for his army to cross the Channel in barges.

▼ HMS *Victory* in Portsmouth Harbour, 1892. The famous ship is now in dry dock and open to the public.

► Nelson explains the plan of attack to his officers before the battle of Trafalgar. His courage put heart into his men: 'I am of the opinion that the boldest measures are the safest', he once wrote.

▼ Thomas Masterman Hardy was at Nelson's side on the *Victory*. He was captain of the ship and a close friend, usually cutting up Nelson's meat for him at dinner.

England, knowing that the great battle was not long off. On 15 September, he sailed from Portsmouth, after a grand farewell dinner on board *Victory*. He had paid his bills and planned next year's planting in the gardens at home. Crowds cheered and wept as he was rowed out to the *Victory*, waving his hat. In the coach taking him to Portsmouth he had written a prayer in his diary, beginning 'May the great God, whom I adore, enable me to fulfil the expectations of my country . . .'

HMS *VICTORY*

THE *VICTORY* had a crew of nearly 1000 men. Their average age was 22. The most experienced seamen were in charge of the huge iron anchors and the sails at the front of the ship that were important for steering. To lift an anchor from the seabed needed the muscle-power of about 250 men turning a winding wheel called a capstan. Topmen (70 sailors to each mast) climbed the tall masts to take in and release the main sails. Other men worked on deck, hauling on ropes. On each of the three gun decks were from 28 to 32 guns, evenly divided between the two sides of the ship. The *Victory* had 104 guns in all. The biggest guns could shoot a ball through oak planks 60 centimetres thick at a distance of 1500 metres.

■ NELSON'S LAST BATTLE ■

THERE WAS REJOICING in the fleet off Cadiz when the *Victory* arrived. Nelson inspired confidence in his captains, his 'band of brothers', and gave them courage. He had told them that their gun crews were better than those of the French and Spanish and that 'no captain could go wrong if he placed his ship alongside that of an enemy'.

ENEMY SAILS IN SIGHT

On 19 October, distant sails were spotted as the enemy fleet left port. Battle was only hours away. Off Cape Trafalgar, a sandy strip of land jutting into the sea, the ships moved very slowly. Nelson placed his ships between the enemy and the safety of Cadiz harbour. The 26 British ships sailed into battle in two columns. Nelson led one line; Admiral Collingwood in the *Royal Sovereign* led the other. The 33 French and Spanish ships formed a sweeping curve.

SIGNAL FOR BATTLE

Nelson ordered a flag signal to be sent to the

EVENTS

1805 *By August, Austria, Russia and Sweden join Britain in the war against France. Battle of Trafalgar and death of Nelson (21 October). In the United States, explorers Lewis and Clark reach the Pacific Ocean after crossing the Rocky Mountains (November). Napoleon is still unbeatable on land. His army defeats the Russians and Austrians at the battle of Austerlitz (December).*
1806 *Funeral of Nelson. Death of William Pitt (January). France defeats Prussia at battle of Jena (October). Napoleon is not finally defeated until the battle of Waterloo in 1815.*

▲ Nelson falls to the deck, mortally wounded, as the battle rages around him.

fleet: 'England confides that every man will do his duty'. The signal officer asked to change *confides* to *expects*. He explained that it would need fewer flags to send.

At midday, the battle of Trafalgar began. The two British columns broke through the enemy line. In a general fight, ships moved close to one another, cannon firing.

THE DEATH OF NELSON

As *Victory*'s guns thundered shot into two French ships, Nelson walked on deck with Captain Hardy. The admiral had insisted on wearing his full uniform, with glittering medals. A marksman perched in the mast-top of the French ship *Redoutable* saw him and fired. Nelson, badly wounded by a musket ball, was carried below deck.

Nothing could be done to save him. He died about 4.30pm, knowing that victory was won. His last words were 'Thank God I have done my duty'. Eighteen enemy ships were captured or destroyed. Admiral Villeneuve himself was taken prisoner.

A HERO'S FUNERAL

The badly damaged *Victory* was towed into Gibraltar. When news of Trafalgar reached London, people wanted to cheer a victory, but instead mourned the death of their brave admiral.

Nelson's body came home in a barrel filled with alcohol. On a cold, clear day in January 1806, his funeral procession moved slowly through London's streets from the River Thames at Whitehall to St Paul's Cathedral. Vast crowds lined the streets to watch in silence. The 'great and gallant Nelson' as *The Times* newspaper called him, had the hero's funeral he had wanted.

▲ Nelson died in great pain but until the end asked for news of the battle.

■ NELSON'S LEGACY ■

TRAFALGAR SAVED Britain from invasion. The British navy ruled the oceans and did so throughout the 19th century. Nelson's death in victory was seen as a national tragedy. More than ever, he was a British hero. Poems and songs were written about him, his picture was seen on plates, mugs, tea trays, and many other articles. There were posters of him in the streets, paintings of his ships and battles, and a wax figure in Westminster Abbey. Streets, public houses, ships, and even towns were named after him.

Nelson's statue stands in Trafalgar Square on top of Nelson's Column – London's best-known monument. The *Victory* is kept by the Royal Navy in dry dock at Portsmouth.

NELSON'S NAVY

Not long after Trafalgar, steamships began to replace sailing ships like the *Victory*, but the 'Nelson touch' is still an ideal honoured in the Royal Navy. Nelson's shipmates admired his courage and determination. They also loved him for his kindness to young sailors nervous of climbing the mast for the first time, or to 'powder monkeys' – lads working as gunners' mates in the smoke and heat of the gun decks.

Nelson had faults: he was vain, stubborn and unkind to his wife. But the sailors who tore shreds off his funeral flag as keepsakes remembered an admiral who treated

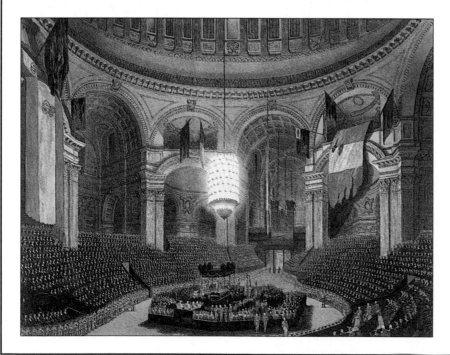

▲ HMS *Victory* is an historic tourist attraction. Visitors can learn about i great admiral and feel for themselve what life was like for sailors who served on the ship.

◀ Nelson's coffin lies in state beneat the great dome of St Paul's Cathedr London, where his state funeral and burial took place.

▶ Nelson's statue on top of its colum in Trafalgar Square, London – the best known of all Nelson's monume The column was completed in 1843 and is 50 metres high.

them fairly. He set a standard for later sailors of all nations to follow and his battles are still studied in naval colleges.

WHAT HAPPENED TO . . . ?

A grateful nation did not take care of Lady Hamilton, as Nelson had asked. She lost her home and money, and fled to France where she died penniless in 1815. Lady Nelson died in 1831. Nelson's daughter Horatia married a clergyman and died in 1881.

Several of Nelson's captains rose to senior rank in the Royal Navy. Captain Hardy became First Sea Lord and governor of the Greenwich Hospital for old sailors, where Nelson's servant Tom Allen ended his days in 1834.

▼ A mother shows her son 'England's pride and glory'. The poet Robert Southey wrote of Nelson: 'England has had many heroes. But never one who so entirely possessed the love of his fellow countrymen'.

■ GLOSSARY ■

ADMIRAL An officer who holds the highest rank in the navy.

AMBASSADOR A country's most senior official representative in a foreign country.

AMPUTATION Cutting off all or part of a damaged limb or body part.

BARON A title held by a member of the lowest rank of the nobility.

BATTLESHIP The largest kind of heavily armoured warship.

BROADSIDE Either side of a ship, along which cannon were ranged on the decks.

CABIN A room on a ship; in Nelson's day only officers had their own cabins.

CANNON A large, heavy gun that fired solid metal balls.

CAPSTAN A revolving post used to pull in a rope or anchor cable that winds round the capstan as it turns.

CLERGYMAN A minister or priest in the Christian church.

COACH A four-wheeled, horse-drawn carriage.

COLONIST A settler who lives in a colony (an overseas land ruled by the colonist's home country).

COMMAND Having control of something, such as a ship.

COMMANDER-IN-CHIEF A senior military officer in control of a country's armies or naval vessels.

CONVOY A group of ships travelling together or under escort for safety.

CUTLASS A short sword with one cutting edge used by sailors in Nelson's time.

DOCKYARD A place with workshops and equipment for building and repairing ships.

DRUMMER BOY A boy soldier or sailor who beat a drum to call crew or send signals.

ESCORT A companion; in wartime, a warship accompanying merchant ships to guide and protect them.

FIRST SEA LORD In Britain, the senior commander in the Royal Navy.

FLEET A number of warships acting together or a division of the navy under one commander or admiral.

FORT A strong building that can be defended against enemy attack.

FRIGATE A fast sailing-vessel with only one deck of guns. Frigates were used as convoy escorts and scouts for a fleet.

GALLEY The kitchen of a ship.

GOVERNOR The ruler of a colony; in a British colony, the monarch's representative.

GUNNER An experienced seaman whose job it was to train gun crews and to look after the gunpowder and cannonballs.

HAMMOCK A length of canvas or net hung by each end and used as a bed aboard ship.

HOUSE OF LORDS The upper house (assembly) in Britain's parliament. It is made up of unelected nobles, judges and bishops. The lower house is the House of Commons, whose members are elected.

INDUSTRIAL REVOLUTION Important change during the 18th and 19th centuries when industries in Britain became mechanised and factory towns grew quickly.

LIEUTENANT A junior naval officer.

MANSERVANT A male servant, usually someone's personal servant.

MERCHANT SHIP A ship that carries goods; a trading ship.

MIDSHIPMAN Formerly the title of the lowest-ranking officer in the navy.

MISSION A soldier or sailor's task; being sent out to do a particular duty.

MUSKET A rifle-like gun loaded through the muzzle and fired from the shoulder.

MUTINY A revolt or uprising against authority in the army or navy.

NAVY OFFICE The government department that in Nelson's day looked after the day-to-day running of the navy.

OPIUM A pain-relieving drug obtained from the opium poppy.

ORDER OF THE BATH An English order or rank of knighthood.

PARSON A parish priest (clergyman) in the Church of England.

PIOUS Religious.

PLANTATION An estate in tropical countries where crops such as bananas, rubber or cotton are grown on a large scale.

POWDER MONKEY A boy who carried gunpowder to sailors firing guns on a warship.

PRESS GANG Group of sailors sent to seize men for service in the navy.

PRIME MINISTER The leader of parliamentary government in Britain and chief minister.

REAR-ADMIRAL An admiral lower in rank than a vice-admiral, originally in command of the rear ships of a fleet.

RECRUIT A sailor who has newly enlisted (joined the navy) or joined a ship.

RECTORY The house where a rector (clergyman) lives.

REVEREND A title of respect given to a clergyman.

SCURVY A disease caused by a lack of vitamin C (found in fruit and vegetables); symptoms are bleeding gums and pain in the joints.

SHIP OF THE LINE A warship large enough to take its place in a line of battle.

SHIP'S BISCUIT A hard, tasteless biscuit (known also as hardtack) eaten by sailors aboard ship.

SHOT Metal balls or pellets fired from a cannon or gun.

SLOOP A single-masted sailing ship.

SPINNING JENNY An early spinning machine (1764) that enabled several threads to be spun at once.

STAGECOACH A horse-drawn coach that carried passengers and mail from one stage to another along a regular route.

TOPMAN A sailor working on the topsails, at the top of the masts.

TRUCE An agreement between enemies to stop fighting, usually temporarily.

VICE-ADMIRAL A senior naval officer, next in rank to an admiral.

WARSHIP A ship with guns for use in sea battles.

WEEVIL A beetle that damages fruit, nuts and grain, and eats food stores.

YELLOW FEVER A tropical disease that causes jaundice (yellowing of the skin).

VICE-ADMIRAL A senior naval officer.

PLACES TO VISIT

Burnham Thorpe,
Norfolk

Chatham Historic Dockyard,
Chatham, Kent

Maritime Museum,
Bucklers Hard, Beaulieu, Hants

Maritime Museum for East Anglia
Marine Parade, Great Yarmouth, Norfolk

National Maritime Museum,
Greenwich, London

Nelson Museum,
Priory Street, Monmouth

Royal Naval Museum and Victory Gallery,
HM Naval Base, Portsmouth

St Paul's Cathedral,
London

HMS Victory,
HM Naval Base, Portsmouth, Hants

■ INDEX ■